T0194762

Drown in the Sun

Danielle Rae Helvie

Cover Art by Nick Rubio

authorHOUSE®

AuthorHouse™
1663 Liberty Drive
Bloomington, IN 47403
www.authorhouse.com
Phone: 833-262-8899

Published by AuthorHouse   03/22/2022

ISBN: 978-1-6655-5564-7 (sc)
ISBN: 978-1-6655-5566-1 (hc)
ISBN: 978-1-6655-5565-4 (e)

Library of Congress Control Number: 2022905399

Foolish young magician
Licks the flame of sovereignty
Whistles scarlet dripping through her teeth
Irrefutable recollection of erotic tentacles
I am sick and sleeping
Penitent but in the order
I have to keep going
Cannot make plans
There is no way to go
When you look up
Some get the bell
Where is that latch I unhooked
Back to my serendipity
Sculpting a dire obsession
Eccentric friends
I summon you
Caressingly lift me

Superhumans
Medieval immortals
This is our Kingdom
The way into ourselves

Wander around the castle
Stop to look and chat
Himalayan blue poppies
Black and calico kitties
Gorgeous and wonderful

Holiness between kisses
Crystals and vintage
From the beginning it is
Until the end it is

Every right and wrong
Eternity is weaving
Gleaming
While glancing
In and out

There was a song
Coming from somewhere not too far
It drifted me away from my visions
The mood reminds me of the memories
I will soon be making
A reality that will become
My situation
Where love and laughter
Are our well known friends
My fortune is one with me
Already attached and in possession
Must I be conscious as I walk
Through these doors
Can I rise
As a shimmering presence
In time on the other side

When I think I have someone
No one comes
When I think I have no one
Someone comes

Always a point of nonexistence
To arrive and exist in
There had to be space to swim

It used to be darker here
For odd reasons
Transmutation
Adds clarity to my invention

Called on the prophets
Within my guided intuition

Behind the scene
The title of the show
Means something else
What is harder to see
I can make it through
To the brink of rays
While I dance in mania
Distracted from revisiting
Howls for alleviation
There is pain to be picked at
Ripped open and stitched up
Just go
I can take this
They will keep me safe
When you cannot
Golden tributes will make a toast
Raising fluid elegance to the ocean

All those adorable exasperations
Mean close to nothing now

I never love you
I never knew you
I never want to

You never came
You pause steady
You wore me down

All those worthy tunes
Mean more than anything

You always play
You created hands
You fly wide

I always love you
I always know you
I always want to

All those glistening hallucinations
Are impending now

Libra season
Maybe it's less about taking
The good with the bad
Or the bad with the good
I've learned recently it's more
They cancel each other out
And that is where the peace is
Balance involves pure trust
Where you almost don't even have to
Acknowledge it to know
It is always here
They give us a gift
It is the same one we had our eye on
A couple hours before
Making up for lost time
But never lost
Meditations in a cocoon
The in-between stages

Goodbyes and hellos
Musky meadow whispers lovely solos
This adventure captured me
And no matter what happens
Its you
We turned us into magic
Something true and something tragic
I will live in this thoughtful colony
Let it devastate
We'll be dancing in fluttering seas
Dip in your pretty wings
Feeling vibrant in these empty spaces
They warned me
But I never listen
Loneliness burns with flares
We can go
Wherever we grow like children
In strange reflections
Past has faded
Future takes me in waves

I love you enough to feel peace
When you are happy without me
Striving to get higher
Alone or Together
Here to be, Here to do
One with me, One with you
Life lines, blood lines
Grape vines and shocking sunshine
I will sink
I will float
I will rise
Unwinding into our embrace
Tried to let you go
But something won't change
Spirits grasp so tightly
Yin and Yang so snug
I love you enough to feel peace
When you are happy without me

Avoid closing in
Until it feels like an abstraction
Thrive in dark times
Make them weary of you
You are too much for this world
And that is the grandest thing
It is our instinct to grab
And hold onto things
We are scared for it to be real
But we do want it badly
It has been so unlikely
And you are just so kind
Say you mean it
How we are more like
The layers of the moon
Than anything else on the third floor

Perform the ritual
It will be excruciating
But that is how it goes

My dimmest has flesh
And it is a lie
I can alchemize
It will be magnificent

Sometimes I am ungrateful
And dwell in what I can't do
Instead of attempting more

Then I remember my strength
I never give up

When items are washed
They have to be squeezed and shaken
Before they are rinsed clear

Inspire me
A breaching stretch
Is it over
I can't see any of us

Where is my love
When is it coming back

Veins in pulsing panic
Yesterday I felt it
I know I saw it
Intensity of glow
Infinity of light

Close my lids and surround
Touching toes without touch
That is myself
The one who knows

I am who encompasses
Within this and out of it
Moon project, star contest

Pushed and pulled away
Going to that state
Having systems to scream erased

There is something about me
I just can't figure out
I patrol by and the fan turns on by itself
They all look at me so funny
As if I am what hadn't been imagined

There are times in life to explain
I beg for the words to describe them
Searched for that one thing
I couldn't destroy if I tried
Turns out I had it all along
I was always inside

I am realizing my wound
It is finally healing
So I can breathe thankfully
Love what is lost
That is how we find them

A lot of the hardest decisions
Turn out to be the right ones

The best way to say we are sorry
Is by actually changing

Sometimes we mistake
Wanting to believe
For actually believing

Nailed your shadow into the concrete
When I am supreme, I am unstoppable
Your insecurities imprison me
I am praying to taste
The base of masculinity
I want to be bold
I want to be whole
I want to be on my own
Tell my story
Before I tell it myself
The mind is silly
Confident but shameful
I get it and you think I don't
Living in a contradiction

All I knew was gone
In this segment of that parallel place
She was speaking me
Into an enlightened attack
I barely made it
I know her from somewhere
A crucial part of me is there
But I woke up back on this plane
Now I am struck
With causes of contemplation
Black holes spinning backwards
A new common dimension
The teachers of curiosity
What do you need from us
I thought we were free

So many miracles
They occur again
You rearrange letters
And arrive
With phrases that make
Everything interesting
Been smoking cigarettes
The people are content
These have been rained on
Not much has changed or a lot has
I'm done with my episodes
There is a sporadic tilt
But that is it and I like it
Unmade beds at the end
Dread in the trash
Oppositions chipping polish
Obtained a level then drifted off
I swam back and tripled
I beat them and the game

I can't stand the way you are
I can't take your look
Explosion
I have no remains
I am not one of them
But I will tell them the secret

I took a dip in the bloody river
Caused some trouble
I have seen them all dead
You are
You are
A detonator
And you are my prey

But I can't be one of them

Everything synchronized
All time high
Material indivisible
In my essential right
Joined with green tender life
Take me into fragments
I am the epicenter with you
We have waited
So don't let me lose
There were happenings of innocence
Gazes that stripped away the trauma
Where can I find you
If you can't hear my call
This weather is matching our personalities
Cold worth shivering
Heat worth sweating
Unstable but merrily wild

The right kind of gloom
Singed into the minute
Kids cheerful and flickering
Giggling sea breezes
It's almost too severe
I might get taken away
Put me to rest
Reel me in
Drip core elixir
Down my throat
All over my complexion

Come to me
It's been awhile

Dear Creator
Tumbling dominos through the replicas
Wonder where I've seen you before

Your world will crumble
Only to show you the sky
Some die at twenty-seven
And some finally come back to life
Heights are a freeway
If you have yourself
You have everything
I find me in the same place I find my faith
You are mostly powerful and have me forever
Your calling will be the only one left
What you use to survive
We are all reaching for it
Covering it up with empty desires
So the farther it gets
Please come back

It is lavishly sustaining
Puzzle with the sky on our image
The clock seems to have stopped
But maybe it was never even on
Must be a memory of perpetual delusion
You were updated and captivating
Withholding my observation
I thought everyone knew
Who was propped astounded
Merging with decadence
It was sincere
Acceptance dissolving terror
In split pupils now
Sure of ourselves
When we are lonely
I yearn for what is boundless

Just because you are out there
And no one can see you yet
Doesn't mean you are not still a star
Let the past become less than you
Time is everfalling
Even now
Each letter is drifting
Beyond
And you are still here
Find joy in caring for yourself
And only be with someone
Who smiles at you
For the same reasons you feel ashamed

I see too much
But cannot cover my eyes
I'd enjoy seeing what you see
The signs that show
The show that glows
And if any of them are coming from
Or pointing to me
Most of the time I don't know
What it is that I want
So I allow the synchronicity
To guide me and translate
My mantle into a flair
I am spending some time now
To have an even greater time later

What we are and what we do
Are the same
Constant flow and motion
I am free in so many ways
But right now I am thinking
One is because I know
No one else is coming to take me
It was exhausting hoping you
Were out there somewhere
Imagining this dance
Took heaps from my soul
Our soul
And now I can just dance
Burst among the musing means
Be true
See through the light in balance
And not lose my mind
To dream and be dreamed of
Is like painting the sky

No need to sink into
The taking shadows
Or burn tense and blind in that shine
Together we are wind and waves
Supply my element like you do
And be my atmosphere
Abrupt in the scorching heat
You are with me in surges
Shifting necessities
Breathing within the breather
But I will suffocate until we are
Tender and on time
How the agreement is knowing

Sight of my ambition
Tagged me
I guess I'm it
You murder me
With the sweetest scent
Overdose on nectar lusting
Heard it on the way
Climb into the cage
Convicted salvation
Drooling passionate rage
Addicted to our synergy
Strange and cooling
Vibes old and new
We can stay here
Wait for the fire
Melt together
Into the ring of water

Blood covered money
And dark chocolate on fire
Craving the smell of it
Comes and goes unexpected
Climax of the film
Soaring over the land
Reacting elements
The perfect potion
Breathtaking moments
Blissful
I feel these wings
They are spread wide
With fields of infinity to see
Bless this hurricane
Fill every drop with my love

Glanced up on the road
The whole planet is in the sky
All deities are the best of friends

They help us discover
The ancient tear
Of quaking romance

Abundances of us
Shatter though the arena
Symbols of an all sided spectrum

Telling tales of halves that
Make amends
Shake hands
Valuing ageless tradition
Religion of quanta

Moving a bit faster now
Turning with my inner compass
On the way from dedication
Sobbed and pleaded
Then you get closer
Why is that
Faith in me
Saying you are me
My unconditional outlet
Standing tall at the forefront
Then crawling low
Reading buried braille
We left our prints everywhere
Market Street teal building affair
Worlds' most wanted
Discussion of the hunted
Waiting with praise
Just another glimpse

We lost our inspiration
What we wrote was empty
But we were in love
Strange pains
The sun in the winter
That soft static
The unspoken-ness
I pretend to lose
I am at least happy I wrote you stories
Sometimes we must be our own angels
Closer to the future
Than to the past
Noticing my traits that amaze
Without me having to show off
Finally not faking this
When I see you see it
The one I read to you
Within our first hour
Is all about us somehow

Uncomfortable elevation
Making a fool of myself

Supporters running away

I spin too fast and funny
Told to never go higher than this
This is nightmarish and familiar

Cherry blossoms surround me
Pulling me conscious, back here

Ground is gold and shapeless

The house we drift into

Tensions tie
In the narrative of denial
A fancy bow
And a mild inked eye
Simplified
A rush gone sure
Minimize
The royal torture
Cold wet glittering dust from above
Coat pearly feathers
And the silkiest scales of skin
Numbers controlling
Thoughts provoking
Things
That
Are
Not
Alone
And
Certain

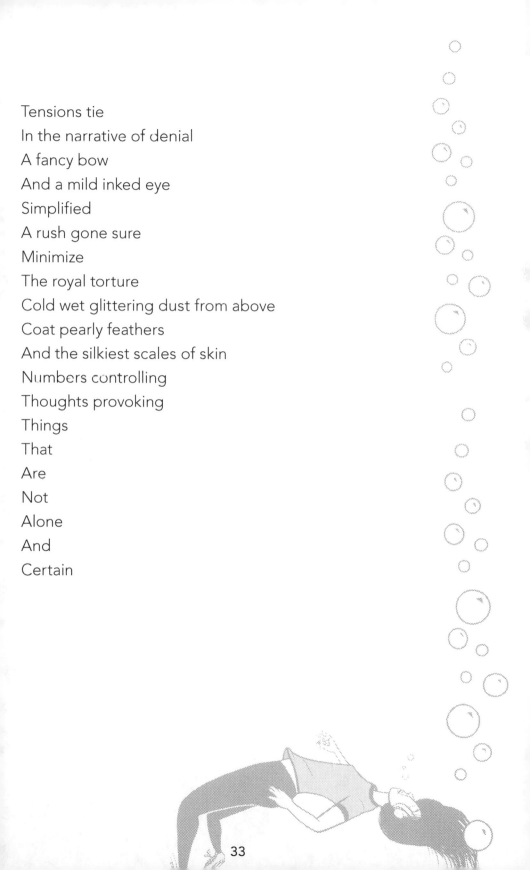

Are you teasing me
Favoring my desire
To keep me close enough
Pondering existence
Mind and body wringing tired
Heart and soul faintly wired
Chances choose me
That is how I relate
Maybe just for them

Those slithers from tongue and lips
After the slide of the wrist
Zoning more and more
Into this warm bind
That stillness shocked every stem
And it is prevailing intact
Desperate to aim aside
Unless of course you are home

Art is the way the world is
Maybe the only real way it changes
Just a phase or just me
If I had to forget about you
And what came with the ride
I would have to never
Ever hear music again
Alibi is chrome like
Starved and drinking tea
File down my teeth
Birth life afterlife
Then birth again
Decide you love this
Being awake and alive
Decide you can do it forever
Experience all incarnations
You cannot unconvince me
Of your adoration
Because it gets deeper and brighter
When I'm in it with you

You are the king of illusion
But mostly of passion

I am the queen of destruction
But only in methods of nature conquering itself

Duality chewing while I peer and squint
We stretch this place we've been put

And yet the one speaks quiet

No fear
No disturbance

Locked in seldom sensation
It is like a carnival
And I still want to know how
You had it in you
Pretend to let me leave
I never will
In that night and in the memory
We deleted them again
If it was a trap
I might be okay with it
Most of what has to be done cannot be sensed
They don't always understand it
When they are in view of themselves
Allow someone to match the critic
Any will do
But make them beloved
For being no walls internally
Is the celebration
Simply and yet consequently us

I have always been the girl
That couldn't control herself
Saying honest uncomfortable lines
Prancing and fleeing away and talking so much
Then being ashamed of the backscatter
It isn't until now that I can admit
I accept myself for it
Because it takes an ethereal quality
To constantly lose yourself
A part of me can recall
Not being able to hold on
But still being held onto
That is why I stuck out
Everytime I attempted to fit in
There is a thrill in joyful negligence
In the practice of countless glints
There it is in the distance

Wandering dreamers
Trickle and twirl
Along buzzing lakes
Over the dirtiest mountains

Carrying us
To courageous fantasies

Silver faded into bronze
Live long or die strong
We can have both

Are you too brave to be alive
And too afraid to just die

Do we go in pairs
Or on our own

What should I get used to

I hope that it's you

Who knows actual truth

None of us really do

To me

There is no point of lighting a candle
If the flame is not in my view

Sure I can take in the goodness
And know it is lit

But out there is what is like my blood
In the fire

Roam in the fires of life
Swim in the depths
Whistle and float along
Count the steps of these hearts

Sadness not madness
I will remember
Internally you are
Mooshy and blue
Just like me
My dearest interlude
Riding in the car
Caffeine on the highway
I never want to get there
To wherever we are going
Let's take this road trip for aye
And disband every bit of damage
And all it has taken

We were conflicting
You said pain makes the music better
I said love lets the music change the world
But how can you get through the pain without
Love
And why would love be so mesmerizing
If it wasn't for all the pain it endures
We are both so true
Those oppositions have come to be the same
You can play through your pain
I can love through my literature
But I need the pain now
And I hope you need the love

Once I hold my wish
In my sweaty tired palms
Darkness begins to fade in
Like irrigated nothingness

Reversing karmic phenomena
Within the cracks
Hovering doors in door frames

Hurt me and keep me
I am scared but it doesn't matter
A voice tells me I am god
But I pray to angels
And the wind that flies them
Whoever or whatever is behind them

They all forgive us for not knowing
We were never alone and yet we are
Separated and combined
Across a shiny rainbow star

Still diving
Glorified
You were trying
A brutal form of affection
While I weep,
Drown
It is beauty
As I turn to my side
Goodnights utter
Paving the way to my remedy
Comfort we created

Would you just kill me already?

No, you kill me!

Cosmos curing
On the verge of extinction
Camouflage and jets
Missions all in the mass
Protector inadequate to abandon
Its offspring of mercy
There is lasting consistence
If you are below a beat
Flowers in the barrels
Smooches on temples
Honoring every animal
The pit or the unimaginable
An ultimatum confronted
Decide to pursue the feed
Within what is balancing

More than love it is
Whatever this is
There is no word to be

Heart stretches
Beyond comprehension
All I do is feel
It is confusing but real

Stay this time around
Don't let me forget again
Help me shed

Because this is supernatural

Most of us are afraid
Of power, of perfection
Of utterly pure reflection

Give that little kid you were
The future they always wanted
I think it is greater to have
Less of what you gave to yourself
Than to have the most
When you got it from someone else
You are getting to where you should be
As if you weren't ever disoriented
Whatever you are is real
Rare and sanctified
Must be guided and protected
Make an appearance in contentment
No more death or fear of it

The imbalanced minds are the ones
That help balance the rest of the world
Or at least the rest of humanity
Friendly accepting ones
Present to me
Numbing tuned in vessels
Valuable enough to inquire
I'm inquired and inspired
Palms revolve currents
Not sure what that is
If you know please tell me
Mysteries withhold awakening
Culture thumping
Threes multiply

Star syndrome and lust for the damned
On the uphill shore, kissing the man
Gulped down his mighty venom
And didn't stress if it could make me ill
Ran my nails along paled softness
As it turns tan and the face changes
Spoke the words, so I said them right back
I ponder the reasons for being invited
And how I knew precisely where to go
Bowing my head
Under the wavened liquid ramada
Then a short climb
Almost like a mirage
And It seemed as though
I just woke up
Remembering a dream
But I was still asleep

Do it electric
While waiting for negative news
Then make that electric too
I don't mind if we are old
When in our disaster again
It takes life
To be in the afterlife
Beside ourselves
Just like we have been
Many many blisses before
It is never leaving
Faultless thoroughgoing
I contemplate in sorrow and hope
I hug your delightful savior
Trillions of unstoppable sequences

It is so rewarding
Where there are doubts
There are also confirmations
They take over
When I feel lost, I am not
Because I can know what to do
And find out what the right choices are
Just by paying attention
And going with what seems like a map inside
Guiding me through and along the outside
Why would I question you
I will just move and listen

Kaleidoscope repertoire
I know what you are when you are silent
Or saying a contrasted word
Learning deepness in this round
There's always something
About where you're from
But you'd like to see everything that is new for you
I want to sleep with every version of you
Write our memories into subliminal messages
While we go through these calendars
We'll call it all then and now
They are not always dwellers
Simplex on the outside
Complex on both ends
On repeat
Gradually restricting me
From my famous worst
I see more darkness than shooting stars
That is why we appear empyrean
And you can't hold on

It came late this year
Unmistakable
Heaven in between us
The one terrifying
If there was another way
We'd all be standing still
That irresistible exhilaration
Feels too good so it must be evil
What else am I supposed to think
I don't have a choice anymore
If only we could know who we are

Pour into the wide windows
The rain of the sun
Implode into a fully awakened state
I cannot speak through the intensity
Take me over completely
Register opens and closes
As a pleasantly heightened jingle
Brings joy to my senses
As I observe
Nothing requires an explanation
Colors and people
Places and sounds
It all comes with the spark

Showing up
Canoodles on every speck
Irises dare despise
However this is
I am in it so long
An end unattainable
Inflictions dearly loved
Span for me to mend misfortunes
Hold our wick in the lantern
This one is already lit
Go ahead and stomp on it
But be careful not to burn
I will be careful as well
Because the journey is rough
And so much fun
Strolling in circles
Reaching into a grasp
Call and rip off the mask
At the very last second

The traveling ghost
Crowd glares at me on the ceiling
They were not amazed or impressed

I am always singled out
The last way to get out
Is to design
A plotted foreseeing
Spellbound obituaries
I can understand it
Because of what I missed

It is all my doing
They are in danger or already finished
Get through this
The other ghosts
Are in the capsule
Raiding for favors
The prize is intricacies
For the architects with spirit over mind

East and West Coasts
Remembrance collide
I can intake you
But I can't decide
Which grip of instances
This aroma reminds me of
Scents are enduring
They are motivating us along
Inner world first
Before your form
It is picturesque
With my eye
Showing the still fact
That all is passing down
Falling through
Except for right now in extremity

In the crispy delighted jungle

Like a miming misfit alliance
Hyper spiritual waves
Come through the production

There is an enterprising circus
That seeps through the terrain

Unlock the entrance

Our pores of poison

Mouth, nose
Eyes, and ears

Evoke

Support my demonic weakness
Weld it safely in what sings on the surface

Coming really close
Sunlight is doing that thing
When it happened before
Drenched in blue and red pigments
It was too much
I knew death
Spoke his name
I beg to overlook

Asking myself
Who did it the most
You ask yourself

I think of us
Sliver of a broken glass mirror
Shattered and tame

Show me all the things
That remind you of me
I want to be the scene
Halloween in the spring
You will be hated for doing
What is right
Our choices will overthrow the law
While dominion is the responsibility to care
Anger can drive
It can drip irresistible beauty
Maybe it is filthy
Intoxicating
And furthermore escapes unconsciousness
In the release we sense freedom
Pleading untouched

To hear your scars
And read your pain
I behave in a way so daring
Somehow we are still alive
Saved on a basis that is now
Irresistible for me to notice
Wishes can seem like sins
When they are magnified
In the front row
On our stage of truth
Not sure who I am speaking with
Welcomings in a hollowed house
Thanks in a filled house
It is interchanging
This unfathomable treasure
Ruling the indecisiveness

Who made us rocket
Here is my soul again
Ancient figure
My validity
Moan in deep
I peer into a galaxy
Scintillation generating
Plentiful and complete
The two hemispheres
And there's that noise
I'm not looking
I had given my control and taken it back
But never froze myself
Remember what it is beneath the marrow
The mind is quieter
In the midst of running light

There weren't consequences
As I was in
Learning the dynamics
Of signals without form
They weren't out to get me
I was wanting them
Chasing the ends of ego
For it to dissipate
I notice now
My eyes are green when I cry
Emerald in stones
And I can officially grieve
Without hankering to see
Because the gruesome trial
Is separating counterparts from the divine

Characteristics we enjoy in others
Are ones we hold ourselves
Why is it such a struggle
To fully enjoy and accept ourselves

It is just a virus
And it has nothing on us but a worn off stamp
You don't have to be cured

Have sex with your own identity
All the way back to the origin
The mirror doesn't do you justice
You speak the language of oscillation

Still here with everstrong remorse
I thought you'd be away forever
Then I found you in that spot
That spot of spark
Where we collide in the middle
Precious and little
Fragile and brightly brittle
Love and infinity are my favorite words
Because of us
I might use them too much
But those are my vows
On the shadiest days of love
In lightened up nights of infinity
Echo of your steps retrieve
Believe in me
Please
Believe in you
I do

Grass is cold
As it neutralizes
The coldest bank in me
Warmth of the afternoon
Brings my ideas to touch
It is not about how many people
Knowing
Who we are
The extension and impact
They will keep up relevant
Choices meaningful and desires blazing
Allowing themselves to be heard
To be made
To be followed with sacred intention

I've been feeling so tired
You've been in my movements
I need for you to come wake me up
And be there when I fall asleep
The happiest I have ever seen you
Is when you were looking at my face
I should have called you an angel
When we met
Instead of you calling me that
If I am one, so are you
You were saving me strong and fast
And still are everyday

What you really mean when you say

I sold my soul
Is
I showed it to myself

I can make it mean anything
An open mind or a pathological liar
It gets too confident either way
If it was any better
The view would sting
Sting my brain
My insides
Good thing nobody knows

We can't understand colors

Art is insanity
Turn your insanity into art
Every type of motion
On an angled ledge
Not able to be explained

The air was clean that night
February something
I try to take a deep breath
But I just inhale the memory
I hear it like the song
Underneath my thoughts
Yellow and Orange
You were going up
And I was going down
There is nothing more precious
Than what we had then
Even if we did it again
This is still only a memory
What am I
If this is what you are to me
For once it is unfeigned
At least you exist

When meeting someone new
I allow them to corrupt my mind
Fill their truth and illusion
In open containers
Never speaking enough
Always saying a little too much
Either way telepathy takes us on
During that day and as we go away
Content once again
As I am alone
Each time back
The serenity is heavier
Earth presses against my feet harder
Majority is not making a sound
Cannot be sprouted from grounds
What is a sacrifice
But to give up flight
And also to condone it

I am all the signs
Black and White
I am every year
Willingly limitless
Apart our soul
Quiet and gentle
Collaborated electric gold
Who are we
Besides what entertains us
What is beneath
Wanting and needing
I am the moon
In love with the sun
Sorting and sharing our beams
Fairies of forgiveness
We are what we become

Retrospect
Hurry and kiss me
I was about to wake up
So you did
From this point on
I know what I desire
Spun my head to them
They rose like roses
Playing in my symphony
Telling me why you didn't answer
Because it's not meant to be
I didn't believe her
But I consider it all
The stench of excess and violence
Polluted cascades
On the stage around twelve
White pinstriped inside
The absolute
The ultimate
You were sleeping too
Said I'm still yours
Even when we break apart

Emerge organically
And stay patient
Not just these bodies
All that gathers
It is all us
We are all stirring
Commander was never here
Just sent another surprise
Without a glitch or compromise
Mad ones innocent and hated
Spirits held so loud
Some aren't meant to escape
Forsaken bottom is gifted
Get down here and bring
Yourselves up with them
All are necessary for this physic
Parties happening where they're least expected
I will let it out until it lets me go

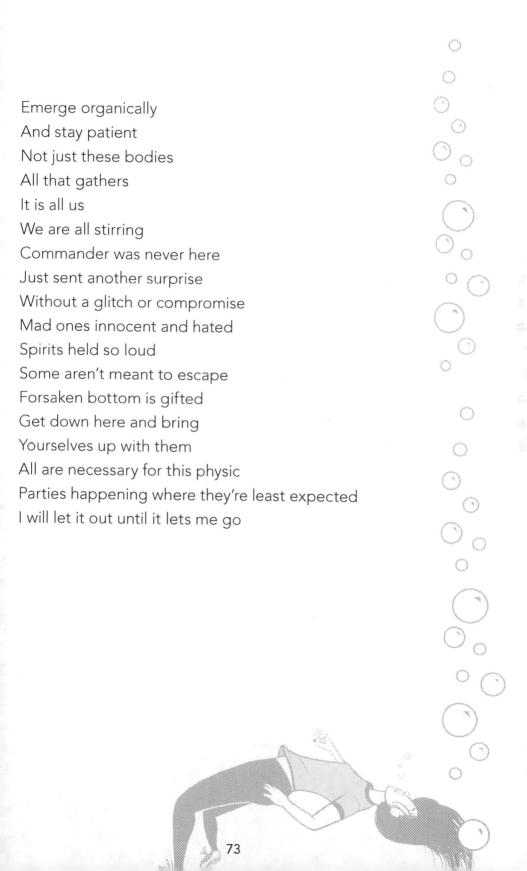

Inside
Calm drive
Roared like the jungle
I was looking for you
We take each other through
The roughest trench
It embodies the kindest parts of us
We switch off holding the flashlight
We share a purple cotton blanket
I tell you to slow down
And then I just run
I roar back to you to just keep it all
How is it that I have lost everything
But still feel as though I always win

I think of the worst things
Nothing but marks
Gleam into a thought
Through some wild eyes
Wild nights
Purpose is not broken
Or meant for something hurtful
Cause I think of the best things
Nothing but dreams
Sleep through the light
Dip into wild fights
Wild flights
Purpose is not given
But meant for something cheerful
Going transformative
Bring me back
While the moon is in the same phase
Show me what is radiant
After the fallen have risen

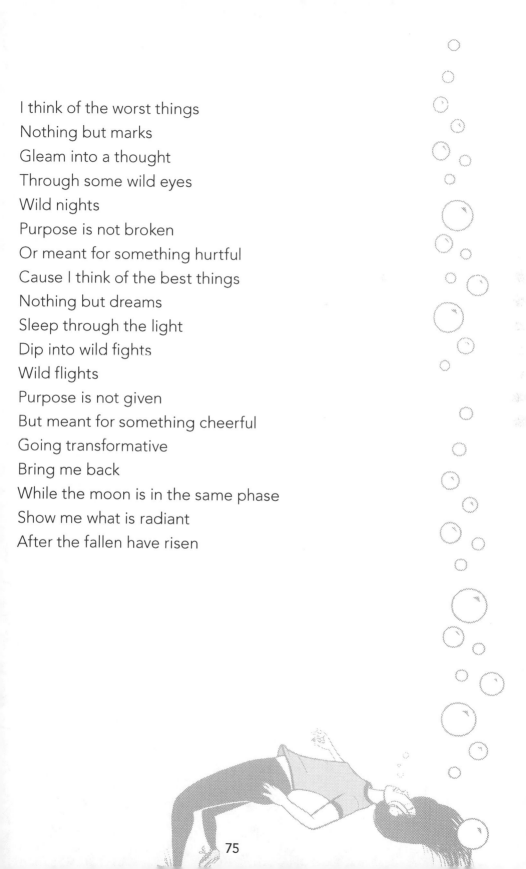

I am whole on my own
Just like the earth
If the sun stops shining
And life leaves me
I will still be ambitious
The raw umbra
Available as a home
Sparkling no matter
In another making
Clouds get silver
And we work in the rain
Our judgment gets cleared
Theories in structures and coloration
Those pillars are there and that is all
They don't mind if they are significant

Feed from it
That
What we cannot understand
Thrive off it
What is held against you
Afraid but with adoration
Pretenders remember
Those days are gone
The mates unravel
Uncontrollable fever
Who can love fearless
Hurting in the process
To reach your own
The greatest revenge
Is always
Your own enlightened success
Then it becomes
The greatest love

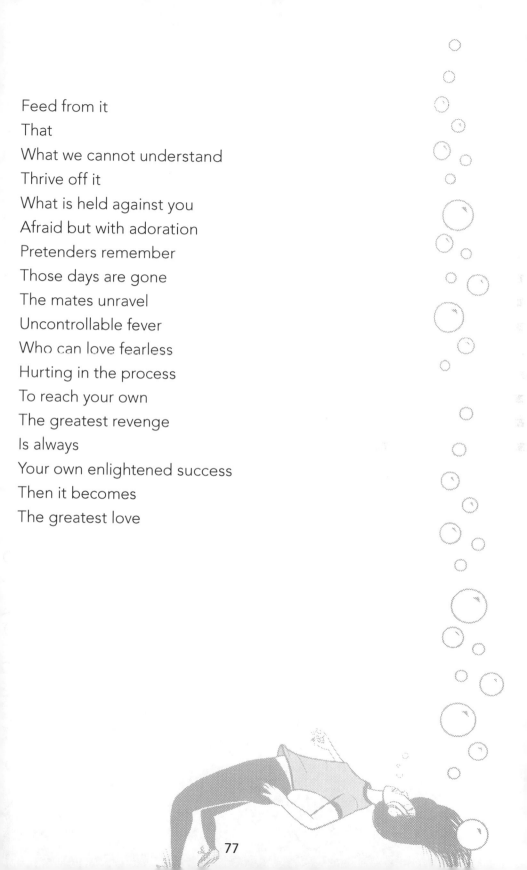

Everyone wants to be a member
Simmering blind
Display in our mind

Mala beaded bracelets
Blanket the pebbled sand
He said it means grand
Not just great
Grand

We ourselves are a lot scarier than our fears
We set our sails and let someone steer

Couple in love
Independent star
Baby being held up to give it a try

Nine in the law of amendments
I haven't learned enough to leave
Or I have learned too much

The breathing heart
Gray with pink horns

Do the deed as it is mentioned
Shift through monumental designs
Go like thunder into the airy dusk

When morning comes
I look around
Chest speaks up and calms down

Edges harden
A cringe of the awakened
Settling into a heightened slumber

Missed marks and dizzy darts
Can you accept the breathing heart
At the time we planned

It was like for one night
We had something vivid and shared
I could convince myself to die
But I won't
Flashbacks of the dream
Scattered unevenly throughout the day
Swimming silk pools
Emotional turmoil
When I can't fly above the water
And it's no one's fault but my own
You only want them
And I know you're blind
I'm blind myself
It's no one's fault but my own
The way I think of you
Now I must seek revenge
On your new city and you

Dandelion

Make me rise
Suggest my song
Give me itch
Pray for me to be
I would love to just be
They said wait 6 years
3 weeks
And 5 days
Runaway
From what makes you unhappy
Come back when you are stronger
All tied up
Become as free as you can

What is me
Floating in here
She is pretty
So lovely
Who is that
Attached and not
Ball of glowing static
Fierce and fantastic
Self is Love
Love is Self
An emotion and something else
Making space around things that are
Worry will only keep me from going far
And what does going far even mean
I will be there along the ride of becoming
Everything

Walks with Goddesses and Gods
Delivering outdoor decor
Long enchanting streets
I can be alone

Now it's time for church
And they know I'm coming
They want to see a show
You don't want to be there
But you'll play

Play for any ears
Bring tears
Streams of gold flake rivers
Leaving fingertips so clear

Convince the friends I am wrong
Gasp suddenly at the sight
Someone was right
We are all Christ

Read my mind so poorly
Can't hear me at all
I levitate to conquer
A seizure through lies of believers
We worship the unknown

You run, I chase
I run, You chase
We both let go

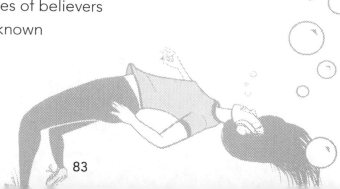

Don't let me die
They want me dead
Who will it be
You you you
Smell my fear
Salty sticky fear
Tipping toward the edge
Drums beating my name
As I stumble into the frame
Leading me
Deceiving dreams
Let go of me
I have to go inside
You wait here
Scream for me
Build me up
Chant until I'm done
Give me some freedom
Inch by inch
Definitive duty
Lightning strikes
I am in
Welcome to the beginning

Printed in the United States
by Baker & Taylor Publisher Services